Flip the Flaps
Planet Earth

Dr. Mike Goldsmith and Nicki Palin

KINGFISHER
NEW YORK

KINGFISHER
LONDON & NEW YORK

Copyright © 2010 by Kingfisher
Published in the United States by Kingfisher,
175 Fifth Ave., New York, NY 10010
Kingfisher is an imprint of Macmillan Children's Books, London.

Consultant: Professor Robert Francis

Distributed in the U.S. by Macmillan, 175 Fifth Ave., New York, NY 10010
Distributed in Canada by H.B. Fenn and Company Ltd., 34 Nixon Road, Bolton, Ontario L7E 1W2

Library of Congress Cataloging-in-Publication data has been applied for.

ISBN: 978-0-7534-6441-0

Kingfisher books are available for special promotions and premiums. For details contact:
Special Markets Department, Macmillan, 175 Fifth Avenue, New York, NY 10010.

For more information, please visit www.kingfisherpublications.com

First American edition April 2010
Printed in China
1 3 5 7 9 8 6 4 2
1TR/1109/TOPLF/UNTD/140MA/C

Contents

Planet Earth

Earth is where we live, a planet that spins through space. If you flew to the Moon in a rocket, you would see Earth in the sky, like a huge, bright disk colored blue and white.

night

Earth

day

Sun

4

1. What is a planet?

2. Does Earth
really spin?

3. Why does it get
dark at night?

.uge ball
that moves
1.

1s
day.

un shines
le of
day there
t where

The path of Earth

It takes one year for Earth
to travel once around the Sun.

After six months, Earth has
traveled halfway around the Sun.

Air

The air is all around us.
We need air to breathe.
Clouds float in it, birds
fly in it, and we call it
wind when it moves.

people climbing

atellite

1. What is air made of?

2. What is the atmosphere?

3. Does the atmosphere go on forever?

birds flying

1. Air is a mixture of gases. One of these gases is oxygen, which we need to breathe in order to live.

2. The atmosphere is the layer of air that covers Earth like a blanket.

3. No. The atmosphere fades away the higher up it goes. There is no air at all many miles above Earth.

People climbing high mountains take air with them to breathe.

The atmosphere

satellite—600 miles up

shooting stars—60 miles up

jumbo jet—6 miles up

7

Life on Earth

Planet Earth is full of life because there is air and water here. Fish swim in the oceans, birds swoop through the air, and many other animals run on the ground or burrow beneath it.

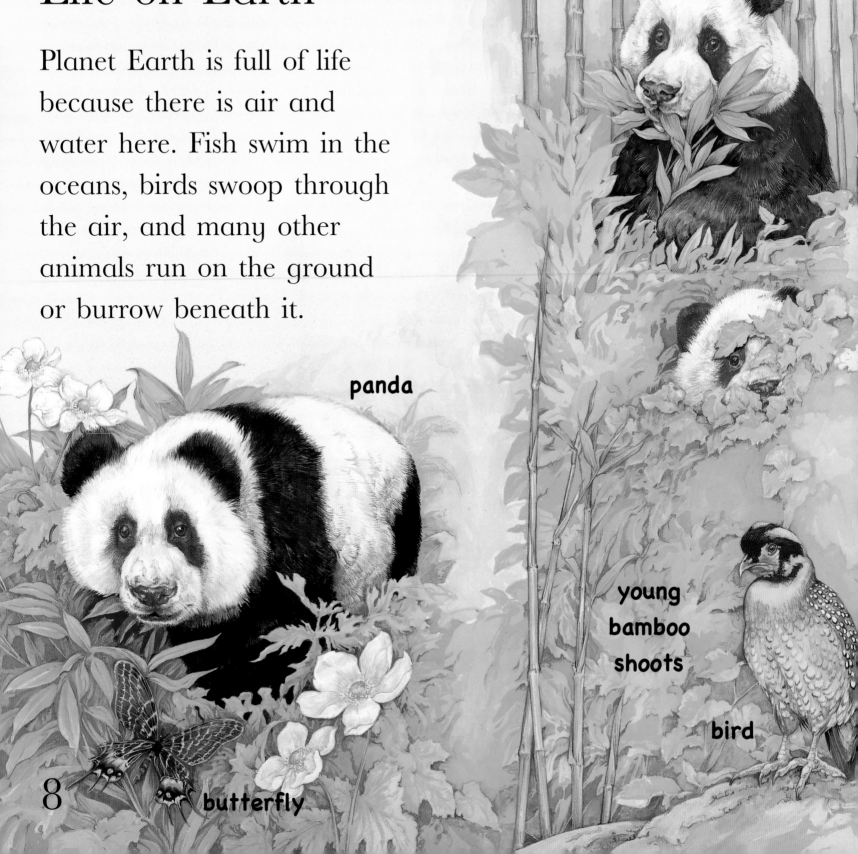

panda

young
bamboo
shoots

bird

butterfly

8

1. Are there living things everywhere on Earth?

2. Are plants alive?

3. What is the largest animal on Earth?

bamboo shoots growing

1. Yes. There are things living in the deepest oceans, on the highest mountains, and even in the hottest and coldest places on Earth.

2. Yes. Plants live and grow—and they breathe, too!

3. The blue whale is the largest animal on Earth. It is as heavy as 2,500 people!

There are many types of life on Earth.

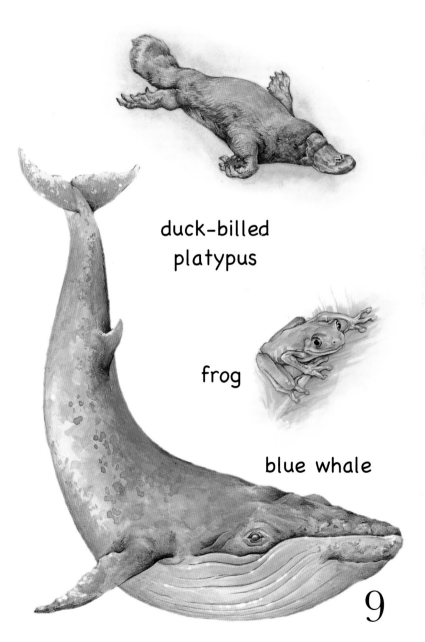

toadstools

duck-billed platypus

frog

blue whale

9

The oceans

Most of Earth is covered in blue oceans of salty water, full of fish and other living things. In some places, the water is frozen into shining white ice.

boat

seal

puffins

10

1. How many oceans are there?

2. What is at the bottom of the ocean?

3. What makes waves?

killer whale

turtle

1. There are five oceans. They are the Arctic, Atlantic, Indian, Pacific, and Southern oceans.

2. The ocean has a floor, with mountains and valleys.

3. Waves are made by wind blowing across the ocean.

squid

deep-sea anglerfish

11

Inside our planet

If you dug a hole under your house, you might find many things: soil or concrete . . . even tunnels or caves! But beneath that, inside Earth, you would soon reach a thick layer of solid rock.

one side of Earth

1. Is it cold underground?

2. What is it like deep underground?

3. What is in the middle of Earth?

mantle

outer core

inner core

crust

1. No. The deeper you go underground, the hotter it gets.

2. Deep underground it is so hot that the rocks melt and become liquid.

3. There is a huge ball of metal, called the core, in the middle of Earth.

Inside Earth's surface layer

plant roots and a water pipe

ancient ruins

fossils

13

Earthquakes

Sometimes the earth shakes and trembles, and huge cracks may appear in the ground. Buildings crack and crumble, and some even fall down. This is an earthquake.

14

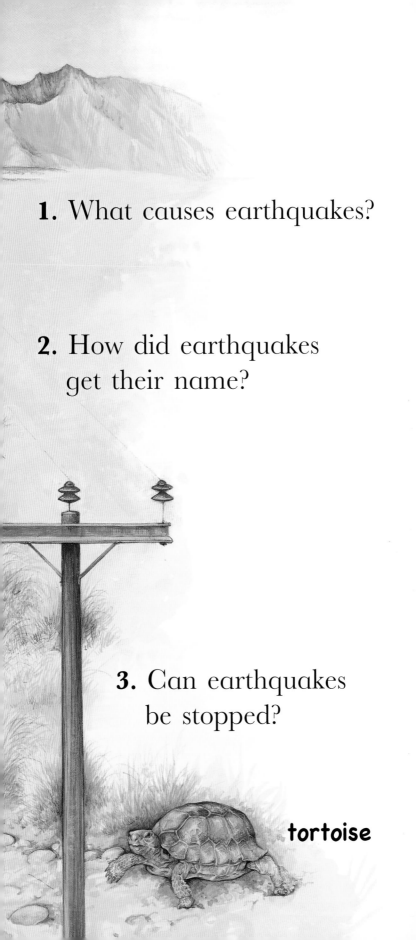

1. What causes earthquakes?

2. How did earthquakes get their name?

3. Can earthquakes be stopped?

tortoise

1. Deep underground, huge pieces of rock slowly scrape past each other. Sometimes they slip suddenly, making the land above them shake.

Most of the time, the rocky plates below Earth's surface move slowly . . .

2. "Quake" is another word for "shake."

3. No, but we can make buildings that will not fall down when an earthquake happens.

. . . but sometimes they suddenly slip.

15

Volcanoes

Not all mountains are quiet and still. Some of them can throw out smoke and fire, like huge fireworks! Mountains like this are called volcanoes.

1. What is lava?

2. Are there volcanoes in every country?

3. Are there volcanoes under the ocean?

1. Lava is very hot liquid rock from deep inside Earth. It sometimes flows out of volcanoes.

2. No. Volcanoes are found only in some parts of the world.

3. Yes. Sometimes the lava from these volcanoes turns into new islands.

An island is formed

underwater volcano erupts

volcano grows larger

volcano cools, and plants appear

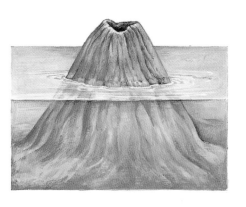

a new island has formed

17

Index